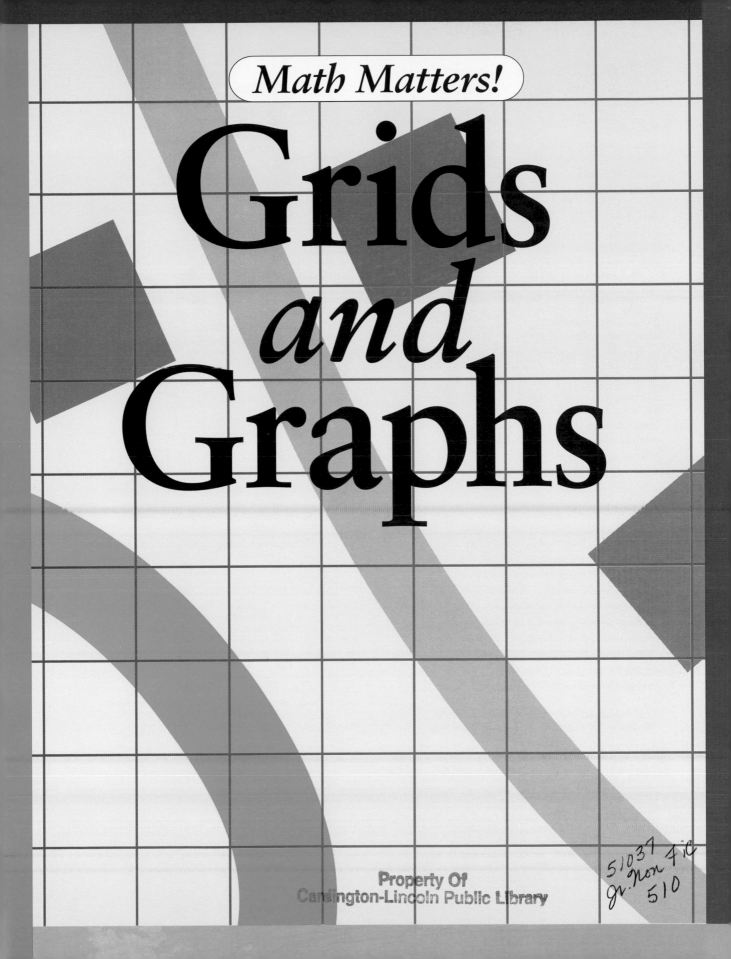

*Math Matters!*

# Grids
# *and*
# Graphs

Look out for these sections to help you learn more about each topic:

Remember…
This provides a summary of the key concept(s) on each two-page entry. Use it to revise what you have learned.

Word check
These are new and important words that help you understand the ideas presented on each two-page entry.

All of the word check entries in this book are shown in the glossary on page 45. The versions in the glossary are sometimes more extensive explanations.

Book link…
Although this book can be used on its own, other titles in the *Math Matters!* set may provide more information on certain topics. This section tells you which other titles to refer to.

**Series concept** by *Brian Knapp and Duncan McCrae*
**Text contributed** by *Brian Knapp and Colin Bass*
**Design and production** by *Duncan McCrae*
**Illustrations of characters** by *Nicolas Debon*
**Digital illustrations** by *David Woodroffe*
**Other illustrations** by *Peter Bull Art Studio*
**Editing** by *Lorna Gilbert and Barbara Carragher*
**Layout** by *Duncan McCrae and Mark Palmer*
**Reprographics** by *Global Colour*
**Printed and bound** by *LEGO SpA, Italy*

**First Published in the United States in 1999 by Grolier Educational, Sherman Turnpike, Danbury, CT 06816**

Copyright © 1999
Atlantic Europe Publishing Company Limited

**Library of Congress Cataloging-in-Publication Data**
Math Matters!
    p. cm.
    Includes indexes.
    Contents: v.1.Numbers — v.2.Adding — v.3.Subtracting — v.4.Multiplying — v.5.Dividing — v.6.Decimals — v.7.Fractions – v.8.Shape — v.9.Size — v.10.Tables and Charts — v.11.Grids and Graphs — v.12.Chance and Average — v.13.Mental Arithmetic
ISBN 0–7172–9294–0 (set: alk. paper). — ISBN 0–7172–9295–9 (v.1: alk. paper). — ISBN 0–7172–9296–7 (v.2: alk. paper). — ISBN 0–7172–9297–5 (v.3: alk. paper). — ISBN 0–7172–9298–3 (v.4: alk. paper). — ISBN 0–7172–9299–1 (v.5: alk. paper). — ISBN 0–7172–9300–9 (v.6: alk. paper). — ISBN 0–7172–9301–7 (v.7: alk. paper). — ISBN 0–7172–9302–5 (v.8: alk. paper). — ISBN 0–7172–9303–3 (v.9: alk. paper). — ISBN 0–7172–9304–1 (v.10: alk. paper). — ISBN 0–7172–9305–X (v.11: alk. paper). — ISBN 0–7172–9306–8 (v.12: alk. paper). — ISBN 0–7172–9307–6 (v.13: alk. paper).

    1. Mathematics — Juvenile literature. [1. Mathematics.] I. Grolier Educational Corporation.
QA40.5.M38        1998
510 — dc21                                                98–7404
                                                              CIP
                                                              AC

This book is manufactured from sustainable managed forests. For every tree cut down at least one more is planted.

# Contents

# Introduction

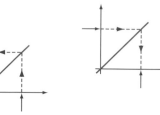

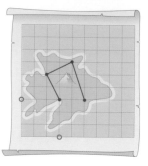

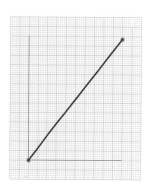

**y = x + 3**

A graph is a kind of map with patterns of crossing lines called grids. It is designed to show you where things are.

The graph can be a real map, which is what you will find in the first few pages of this book, or it may be a mathematician's map, in which case the grid is drawn on graph paper. You will find mathematicians' graphs later in the book.

Using a graph, you can find your way around or convert between different kinds of units. For example, you can convert between metric units and imperial units. You can also convert between currencies. With a little more skill, as this book will

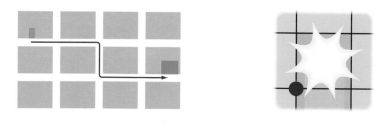

**(1,8)  (7,7)  (1,5)  (1,8)  (5,5)  (7,7)  (2,3)**

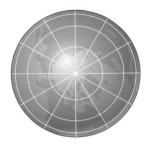
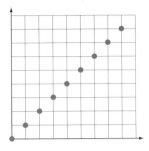

$y = 2x$

show, you can convert between temperatures in Fahrenheit and Celsius.

You can use a graph to solve problems and even predict the future.

Making graphs has only a few simple rules. There are also some smart tricks that save time.

You will find that by following the simple stages in this book, it will be easy to learn all about graphs. Each idea is set out on a separate page, so you can always refer back to an idea if you have forgotten it.

Like all of the books in this mathematics set, there are many examples. They have been designed to be quite varied because you can use mathematics at any time, any place, anywhere.

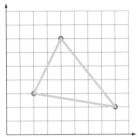

(−5,−2)

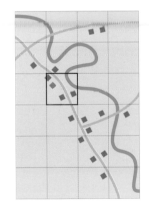

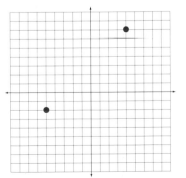

| x | y |
|---|---|
| 0 | 0 |
| 1 | 3 |
| 2 | 6 |
| 3 | 9 |

# Finding your way around

If you are going to give someone directions, you need to have a way of telling them how to move. For example, if you wanted to tell someone how to get from your home to your school, you might say: "Go two blocks straight down the road, then turn right. Walk one block more, then turn left. Go along two more blocks, and there is the school on the left."

## Mental map

It is easy to follow these instructions because the streets are already laid out as blocks. As you read the description above, you may have had a kind of map in your head. Let's see what this mental map might look like if it were drawn out.

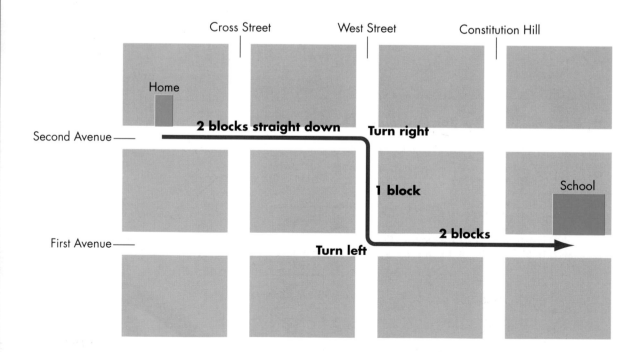

## Directions

Can you see how the description of the journey from home to school gives two important pieces of information? It gives the distance of each "leg" of the journey (two blocks, etc.) and the direction (turn right, etc.).

Now look at this diagram below. It is the same route with the blocks taken away.

Home

School

How do you give someone directions now? Not so easy is it?

There are many cases when people need directions, and there are no local landmarks around to help. For example, sailors and airline pilots often move in the dark or in midocean where there are no landmarks to help.

This is where the use of a grid of lines comes in to act as a reference, as you will see on the next page.

**Remember...** We use reference lines all the time, although we don't always realize it.

### Word check

**Map:** A scale drawing of a place.

**Mental map:** A map of a place that you know well and that you keep in your head.

# Grids

Have you ever wondered how sailors and pilots know where they are at night or when there is no land in sight? They use a clock, a compass, and an "invisible" set of crossing lines – a grid. Here is what the lines do.

## Latitude and longitude

Travelers have always wanted to know where they are and the shortest way to their destination. But, as we know, some sort of guideline, such as the street pattern of a city, is needed to help them do that.

The most famous set of guidelines are those we use for finding our way around the world. They are a set of east-to-west circles called lines of latitude and a set of north-to-south circles called lines of longitude.

You can think of them as invisible lines drawn over the earth. No matter where we go, we can find out our position using these lines.

## Degrees

Lines of longitude and latitude are marked off in degrees. This is because they are really circles, and there are 360 degrees (360°) in the full turn of a circle.

Book link... To find more about the properties of circles and spheres, see the book *Shape* in the *Math Matters!* set.

For more information on degrees and angles see the books *Size* and *Numbers* in the *Math Matters!* set.

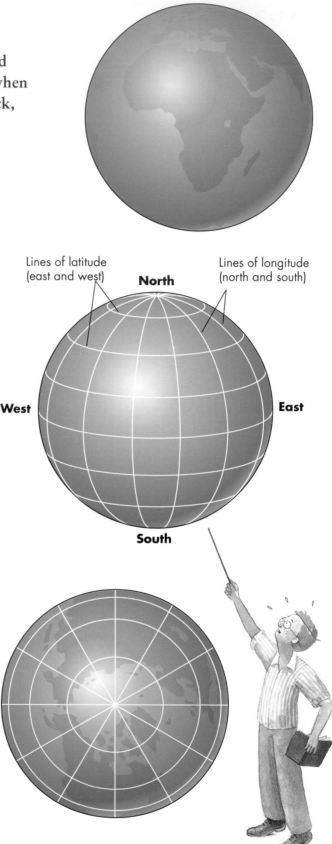

Lines of latitude (east and west)

Lines of longitude (north and south)

**North**

**West**

**East**

**South**

# Where in the world?

Maps are pictures of the globe spread out onto flat sheets of paper. You can see one below. Notice that the lines of longitude and latitude have been carried onto the map and that they now make a kind of grid pattern with the lines crossing at right angles.

Anywhere in the world can be located using these grid lines. Some cities have been marked so you can see how the grid is used. Make sure you understand exactly how we got the numbers.

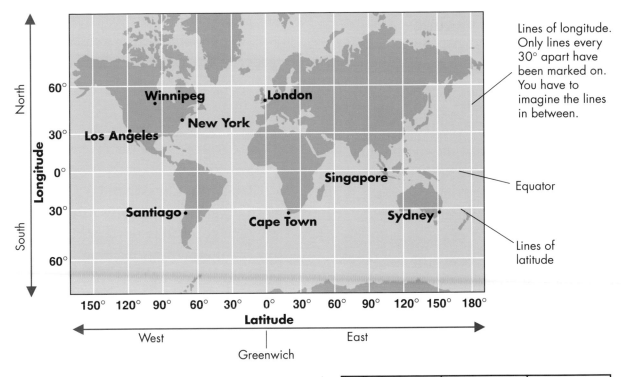

Lines of longitude. Only lines every 30° apart have been marked on. You have to imagine the lines in between.

Equator

Lines of latitude

## Word check

**Degree:** A small part of a complete turn. There are 360 degrees in a complete turn.

**Grid:** A pattern of lines that cross at right angles that is used to make it easier to set out your work.

**Latitude:** Lines drawn on a map or globe parallel to the equator. They are measured in angles north or south, for example, 52°N.

**Longitude:** Angles that mark the distance of places east or west of Greenwich, England.

**Right angle:** An angle that is exactly a quarter of a complete turn.

| City | Longitude | Latitude |
|---|---|---|
| London | 0° E | 52° N |
| New York | 74° W | 41° N |
| Los Angeles | 118° W | 34° N |
| Sydney | 151° E | 34° S |
| Cape Town | 18° E | 34° S |
| Singapore | 103° E | 1° N |
| Winnipeg | 97° W | 49° N |
| Santiago | 71° W | 33° S |

**Remember...** You must have a set of crossing reference lines if you are to give someone your position. On a globe they are called lines of latitude and lines of longitude.

# Using grids

Grids can be very useful for locating places on a map

## Finding your way to the treasure

The map on page 11 was made by long-dead Captain Pegleg to remind him of where he buried his treasure.

Look at the instructions on the right and at the map. The first instruction is "Land at 3,3."

Now where is that?

To find out, you need to find the number 3 on the bottom number line.

It has been marked with a blue ring. Notice that it is three lines across.

Now find the number 3 on the upright number line of the map. It has been marked 3 lines up from the 0 on the map with a pink ring.

Now use a finger to follow the first point 3 up and another finger to follow the second 3 right until your fingers meet. As you can see, this is Sandy Cove, a good, sheltered natural harbor.

So the captain used two numbers separated by a comma to tell him exactly where the landing spot was.

Now for the journey inland.

The next point is 2,5.

Use the same method to find it. First move 2 along the bottom number line, then 5 up (some people remember this order by saying to themselves "along the corridor then up the stairs." Use it if it helps). This is Scarface's Grave, the place where Scarface fought Captain Pegleg and suffered the consequences.

Now to 4,6.

Repeat the same method, along first, then up. This is Hanging Rock, a good vantage point to make sure that no other ships are approaching.

Finally, down to 5,3.

Using the same method again, go along, then up to get to Devil's Hollow, the place where the treasure lies buried.

So now it should be easy to find Captain Pegleg's treasure, except that he didn't say what the real name of the island was. What a pity!

| Instructions | |
| --- | --- |
| Land at | **3,3** |
| Go to | **2,5** |
| Go to | **4,6** |
| The treasure is at | **5,3** |

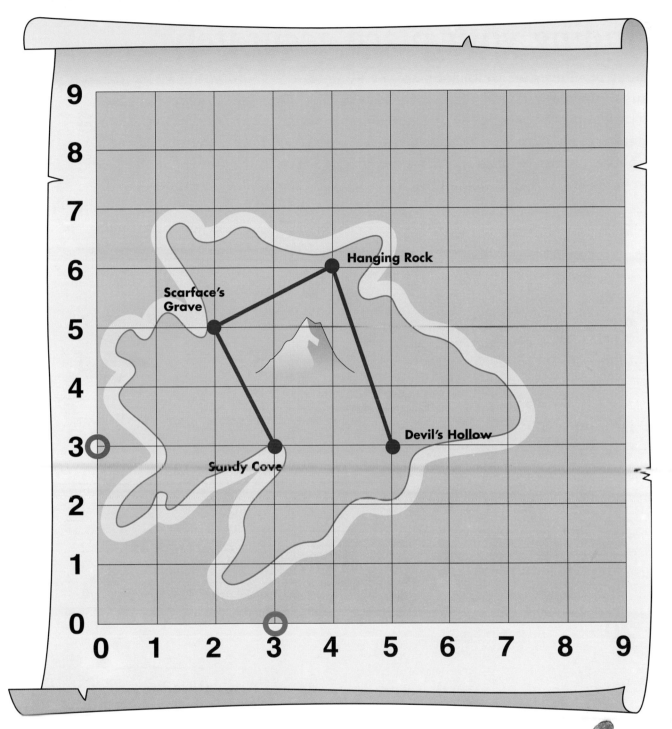

**Remember...** Find your way around a map using pairs of numbers. Use the jingle: "along the corridor and up the stairs" to remember the order of the numbers.

# Finding your place accurately

On the previous page we found places by using pairs of single-digit numbers. In fact, this wasn't very accurate. What happens, for example, if we want to find a place where the lines didn't cross?

This is the case with this next map, which shows part of a town near a river.

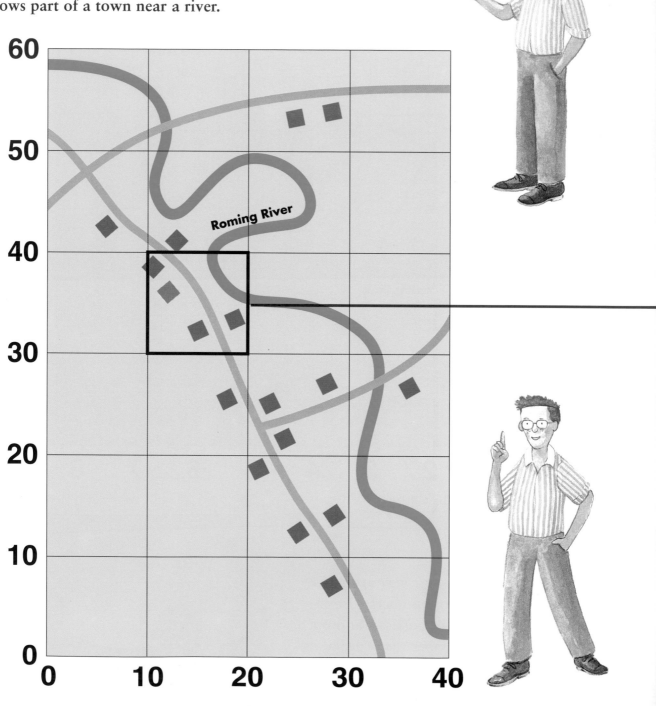

Roming River

Suppose you lived in the house shown in pink on the map. You have some friends coming to visit you, and they have a map, so you can give them the numbers they need to find where you live.

We can do this by imagining each grid square enlarged with more grid lines inside as shown below. This is just the same as seeing a ruler with units and tenths marked in between. Now your house is **1** large and **2** small lines across and **3** large and **6** small lines up. So its position is **12,36**.

Your house does not lie on any place where the main grid lines cross. Saying "<u>near</u> 10,30" is not good enough because there are several houses that this description could fit. We need to be more accurate.

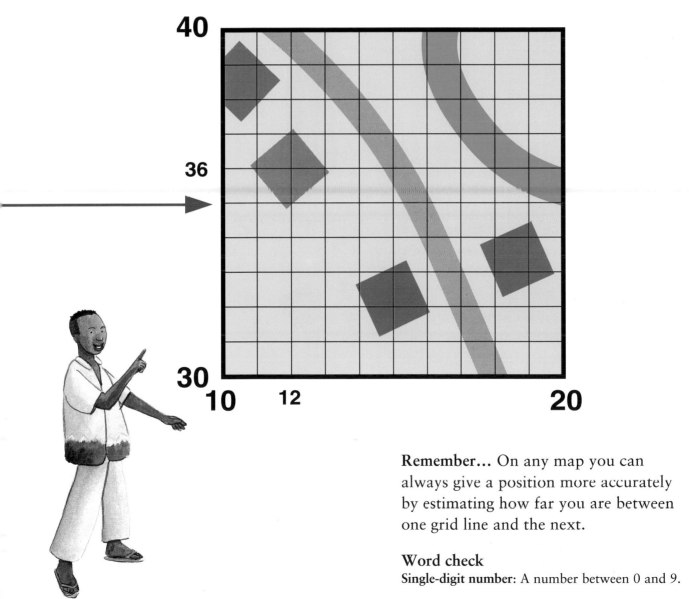

**Remember…** On any map you can always give a position more accurately by estimating how far you are between one grid line and the next.

**Word check**
**Single-digit number:** A number between 0 and 9.

# Battleship coordinates

Coordinates are the numbers that you use to find a place on a grid.

As you have seen from the previous pages, coordinates use the number from the bottom line or horizontal scale first, and the number from the upright line or vertical scale second, with a comma in between. A pair of numbers such as (5,3) is called a pair of coordinates. They must be in the right order. The coordinate (3,5) is another position than the coordinate (5,3). Notice that coordinates are usually enclosed in parentheses.

## Battleships

Here is how a game of battleships could be played over the telephone, making use of coordinates since the players cannot see each other's map.

Each player draws an ocean map on a numbered grid **10** squares across by **10** squares up. There could be some land or islands if you wanted. But players must mark the position of a battleship, a submarine, a destroyer, and an aircraft carrier. This is their own "fleet."

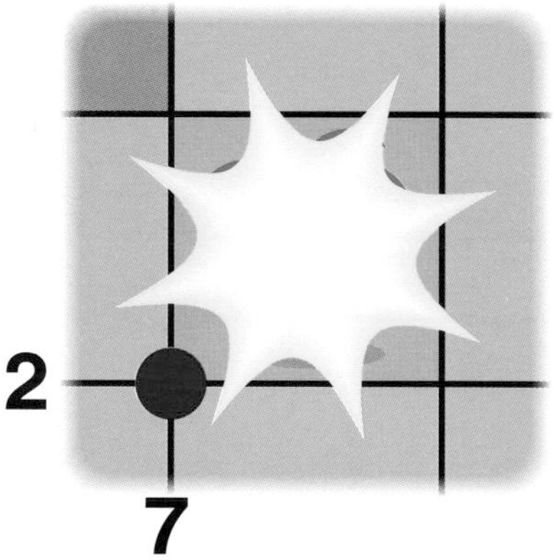

Then the first player sends in an imaginary squadron of aircraft to attack a square on his opponent's map (which he cannot see, of course) by calling out, for example "(5,3)," meaning the square above and to the right of (5,3), as the diagram shows.

The opponent replies: "island," or "miss," or "hit" if the square contains one of the defending fleet. They play the next round the opposite way. The winner is the one who destroys all of his opponent's fleet first.

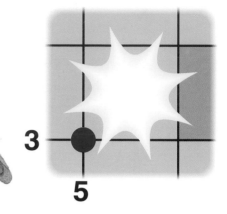

**(5,3) Miss!**

3

5

**(7,2) Island!**

2

7

**(6,4) Hit!**

4

6

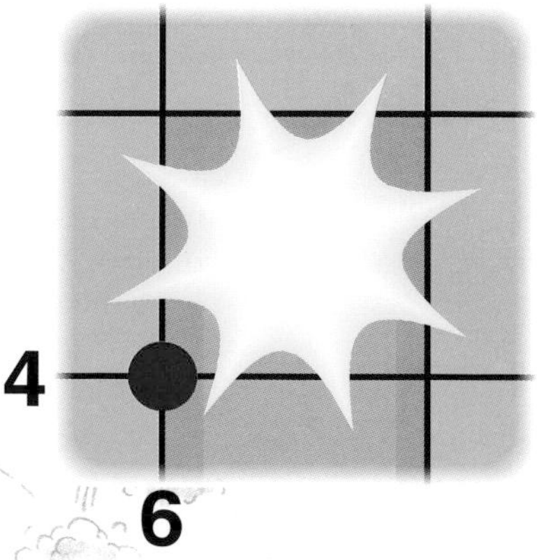

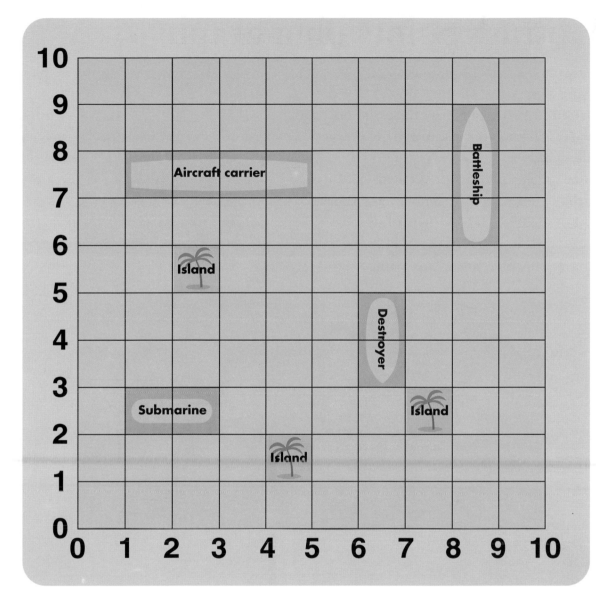

**Remember ...** The order you find coordinates is always <u>Across</u> and then <u>Up</u>; alphabetical order.

**Also...** You can probably think up many games to play with coordinates. Chess has its own scheme of coordinates (which is why players say "pawn to king's rook 4" and so on), but you can also play it using coordinates (king moves from square (2,3) to square (2,4), for example).

We will see how to use coordinates to give data on the size, shape, and position of triangles and lines on later pages. Good math is when you can find lots more uses for an idea.

**Word check**

**Coordinates:** The pair of numbers that tells you the position of a point on a graph. They are usually enclosed by parentheses.

**Horizontal:** Level and flat, like the surface of still water.

**Vertical:** Upright, perpendicular to the horizontal.

# Plotting points on a graph

A graph is a kind of map showing you where things are. Graphs always have two **number lines** that are used to hold the scales. Each of these number lines is called an **axis**.

In mathematics the horizontal number line is called the "x"-axis, and the vertical number line is called the "y"-axis.

We can show the position of any point on a graph using these two number lines, just as we have done on the maps on the previous pages. Any point on this kind of position graph is shown by coordinates as before; the first number tells us how far in the x direction the number is from 0, and the second number tells us how far in the y direction the number is from 0. They are always put in the same order, x value before y value, separated by a comma and enclosed in parentheses.

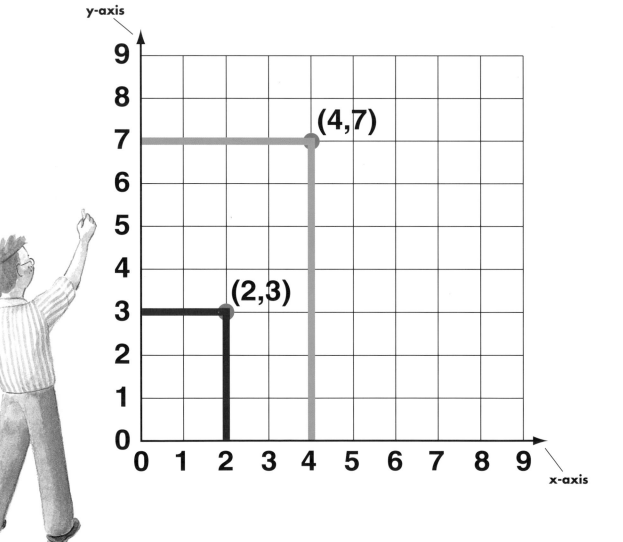

So (4,7) is a point 4 units from 0 in the x direction and 7 units from 0 in the y direction.

If we are given a set of points, we can plot them on a graph and join them up. In this case we have produced a triangle made of the points (2,3), (4,7), and (8,2). So now we can see how to draw a triangle given only the coordinates of the three points.

**Remember…** The order for coordinates is always alphabetical: (horizontal,vertical), (x,y), or (across,up).

**Word check**
**Axes:** The zero lines on a grid. The x-axis is across. The y-axis is up.

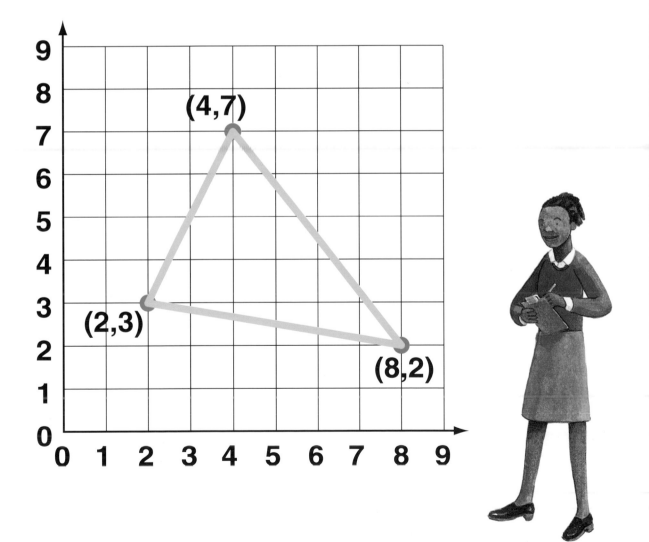

# Secret coordinate codes

Coordinates are called "ordered" pairs of numbers because the order that they appear in matters. You can use coordinates to find hidden shapes and even words. But if you don't get the order right, you will never find the answer! Here are some examples.

## Hidden words

You can hide names on a graph by scattering them all over the graph. You can then give someone the coordinates to find the letters and work out what the word means.

In this case the coordinates of the letters are:

## (1,8)  (7,7)  (1,5)  (1,8)  (5,5)  (7,7)  (2,3)  (8,5)

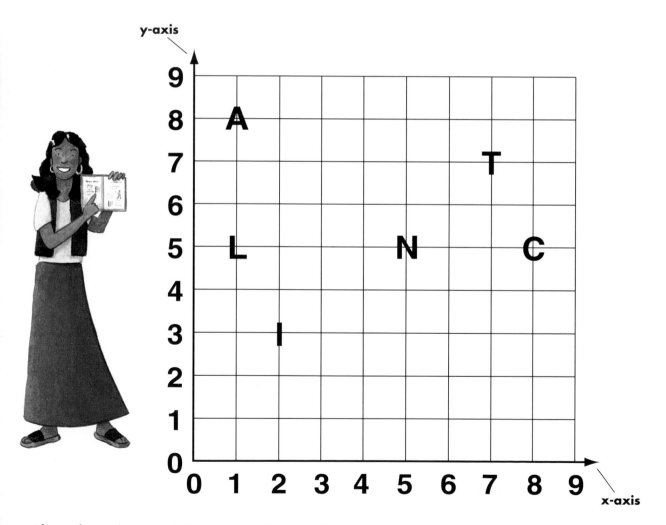

If you have followed them around correctly, you will have spelled out a geography word.

Answer: The word is Atlantic

## Hidden shapes

You can also give coordinates of a shape that people can only see when they have drawn it using coordinates. Here is the shape of a letter "T" drawn in coordinates. The coordinates are:

## (2,6) (4,6) (4,1) (5,1) (5,6) (7,6) (7,7) (2,7) (2,6)

Notice that the starting and ending coordinates are the same.

**Remember…** Coordinates always come in pairs separated by commas. You must get the order right to find the coordinate correctly.

### Word check

**Ordered pair:** Any pair of things (such as coordinates, for example) in which the order matters.

**Pair:** Two things that match up in some way.

# Minus coordinates

Sometimes it is important to be able to plot numbers less than zero. These are called minus numbers.

To do this, we need a graph where the axes don't just start from zero but cross at zero. Compare the graph below with the one on page 18 to see the difference. This means that the graphs we have used before are only the right-hand top part of this graph.

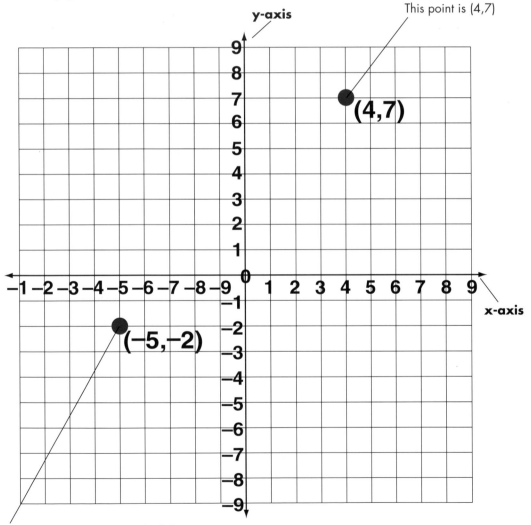

This point is (4,7)

(4,7)

(−5,−2)

This point is (−5,−2) because it lies to the left of the y-axis and so is a minus number on the x-scale and because it is below the x-axis and so is a minus number on the y-scale.

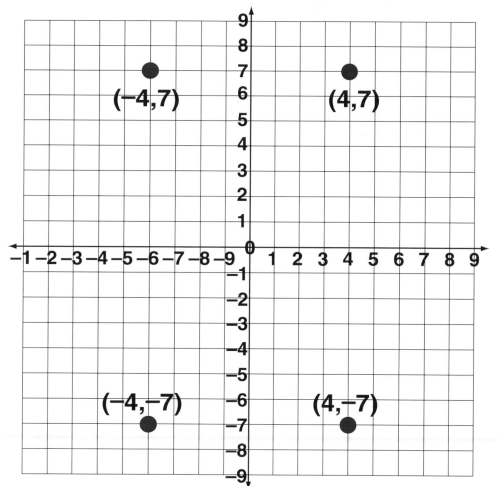

Look at the four dots on the graph above and see how the coordinates are connected. Any number to the left of the vertical axis or below the horizontal axis has a minus sign in front of it.

**Remember...** The sign before the number tells you which quarter of the graph to look in. A minus before the first number tells you to look to the left of the y-axis (vertical axis); a minus before the second number tells you to look below the x-axis (horizontal axis).

### Word check

**Minus numbers:** The numbers that fall below zero on a number line (scale). Minus numbers or zero cannot be used for counting, only for measuring things like temperature. Minus numbers are also called negative numbers.

**Book link...** To find out more about minus numbers, see the books *Numbers* and *Subtracting* in the *Math Matters!* set.

# Finding patterns in coordinates

Sometimes you can see patterns in coordinates. Look, for example, at the coordinates here:

## (0,0) (1,1) (2,2) (3,3) (4,4) (5,5) (6,6) (7,7) (8,8)

In each case both numbers are the same. As you go along the line, you see the numbers go up evenly, 0 to 1 to 2, and so on.

This is what the pattern looks like when plotted on a graph.

**Coordinates are usually easier to see when set out in a table like this:**

| x | y |
|---|---|
| 0 | 0 |
| 1 | 1 |
| 2 | 2 |
| 3 | 3 |
| 4 | 4 |
| 5 | 5 |
| 6 | 6 |
| 7 | 7 |
| 8 | 8 |

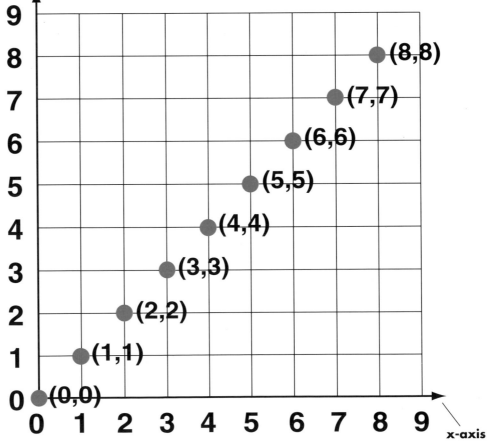

## A straight line rule

Now, if we join up all the points we have plotted, you can see that they form a straight line. You can now use the straight line to see that the value of any point on the line will always have an x value the same as the y value. For example, look for (9,9) at the top right of the graph. You can also imagine this line going on forever, so that if we drew the graph large enough, we would find a point (1,000,1,000) or even (1,000,000,1,000,000) and so on.

**Remember...** The line is continuous. It does not go up in jumps or steps simply because we only mention whole number coordinates. Check that (½,½) and (1½,1½) are on the line, too.

### Word check
**Continuous:** A number scale that increases smoothly, without jumps or steps.

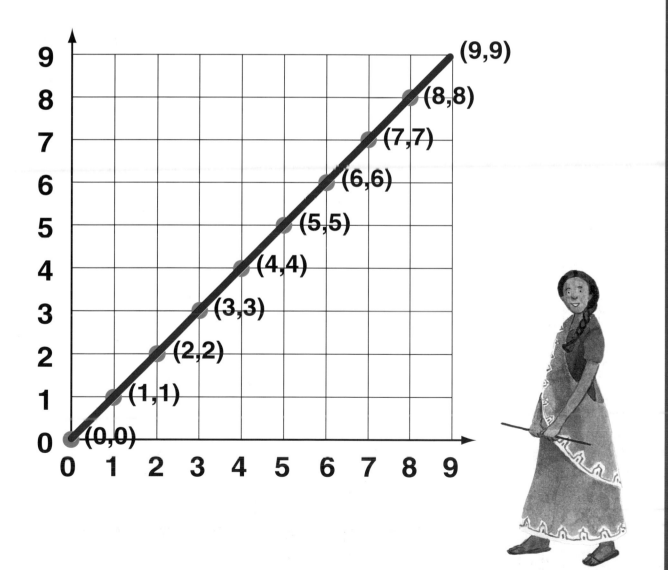

# Line equation

Let's look again at the line we have drawn on page 23. Every x-value (the first number in the parentheses) is matched by the same y-value (the second number in each parentheses).

If we wanted to write a general rule for this, we could put:

## y = x

Any number that you write down instead of x will give you a value for y. So, writing 4 instead of x gives y = 4, and the coordinate is (4,4). This is an equation because it has two balanced items on either side of an = sign. It is the equation of a straight line. Notice that one of the pairs of coordinates on this line is (0,0), so the line cuts right across where the axes meet.

Here are two more tables of coordinates and the lines that can be drawn through their points.

| x | y |
|---|---|
| 0 | 0 |
| 1 | 2 |
| 2 | 4 |
| 3 | 6 |
| 4 | 8 |

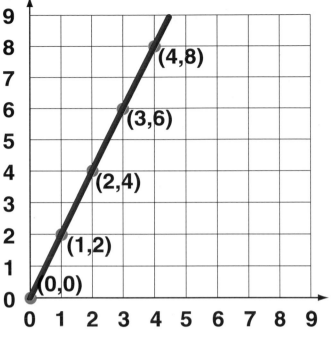

The line equation is:

$$y = 2x$$
$$y = (2 \times x)$$

Notice that this line is 2 times as steep as the line on page 24.

| x | y |
|---|---|
| 0 | 0 |
| 1 | 3 |
| 2 | 6 |
| 3 | 9 |

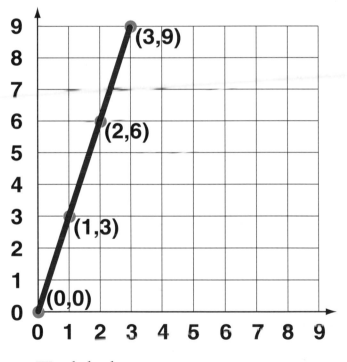

The line equation is:

$$y = 3x$$
$$y = (3 \times x)$$

Notice that this line is 3 times as steep as the line on page 24.

**Remember...** The bigger the number that x is multiplied by, the steeper the slope of the line.

## Word check

**Slope:** A surface or line that is not level. How much (or steeply) it goes up is measured by the ratio UP:ACROSS.

**Equation:** A number sentence using the = symbol, telling us that two different ways of writing a number are the same. For example, 2 + 2 = 4 and 9 − 5 = 4.

# Lines that do not pass through zero

If you look back over the previous pages, you will see that the lines we have plotted all pass through zero. Mathematicians call the point (**0,0**) – the origin.

Lines do not have to go through the origin. Here are some coordinates that produce a line that passes to one side of the origin.

**(0,2) (1,3) (2,4) (3,5)**
**(4,6) (5,7) (6,8) (7,9)**

Notice that in this case the line passes through the y-axis 2 units above the origin at (0,2).

If you compare this line with the graph on page 22, you will see that the slope of the line is the same as the slope of the line on the graph on this page. All we have done is to push it up by 2 units, so that, for example, when x = 0, y = 2 and when x = 4, y = (4 + 2).

This gives us the equation for the line:

$$y = x + 2$$

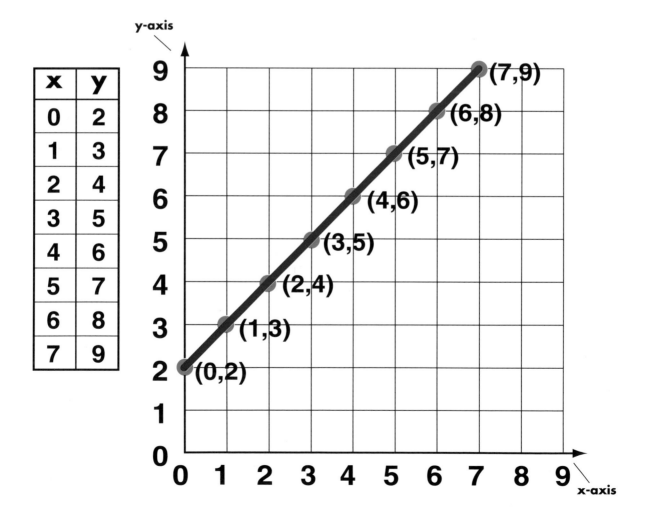

| x | y |
|---|---|
| 0 | 2 |
| 1 | 3 |
| 2 | 4 |
| 3 | 5 |
| 4 | 6 |
| 5 | 7 |
| 6 | 8 |
| 7 | 9 |

Now, in this case the line passes through the y-axis **3** units above the origin at **(0,3)**. Look at the table of coordinates and see that each y number is **3** units more than the x number. So the equation is:

$$y = x + 3$$

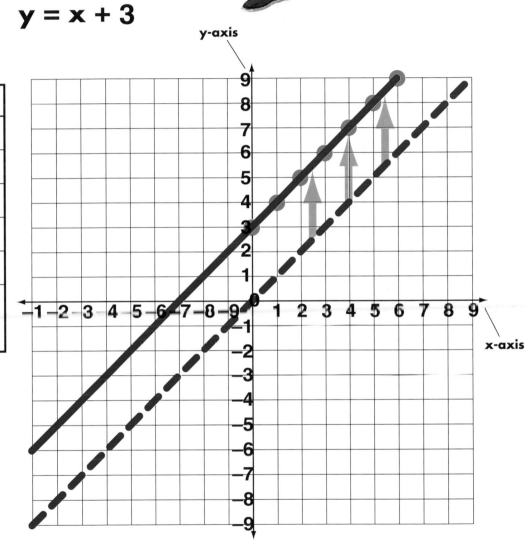

| x | y |
|---|---|
| 0 | 3 |
| 1 | 4 |
| 2 | 5 |
| 3 | 6 |
| 4 | 7 |
| 5 | 8 |
| 6 | 9 |

**Remember...** If a line has a "+ number" in its equation, it does not go through the origin.

## Word check

**Intercept:** The point where a line graph crosses the y-axis. It is the amount the line is lifted above a parallel line through the origin.

**Origin:** The point where the axes of a graph cross.

**Parallel:** Parallel lines are lines that will remain the same distance apart forever.

# Making conversion graphs

We can use a straight line graph for converting from one thing to another, for example, between one currency and another, or for converting between metric and imperial units.

These are the steps that you need to follow to prepare any conversion graph. In all cases graph paper is required.

**Step 1:** The conversion we are going to make is between liters and gallons. For this we need to know that:

## 1 gallon = 4.5 liters

Let's choose our conversion graph to work up to **20** gallons, the sort of range you would need when filling a car tank with gas.

We can now see that because 1 gallon = 4.5 liters, then 10 gallons = 45 liters, and 20 gallons = 90 liters.

This also gives us our first point on the graph. 20 gallons = 90 liters is written as the point (20,90).

**Step 2:** We will need to draw two scales on the graph paper

Put gallons along the bottom, and liters going up. Arrange for each little square to stand for **2** units. The scales do not have to be the same on each axis.

Plan to make the graph as big as you can fit onto the paper.

**Step 3:** Two points are enough to position a line. So, 0 gallons = 0 liters, use the point (0,0). This is the origin.

Now use (20,90) as the second point.

Draw a straight line through these two points as shown.

**Step 4:** Having made the conversion graph, we can now use it. The diagram below shows you what to do. To find out how to use other conversion graphs, turn to pages 30 and 31, 32 and 33, 34 and 35, and 36 and 37.

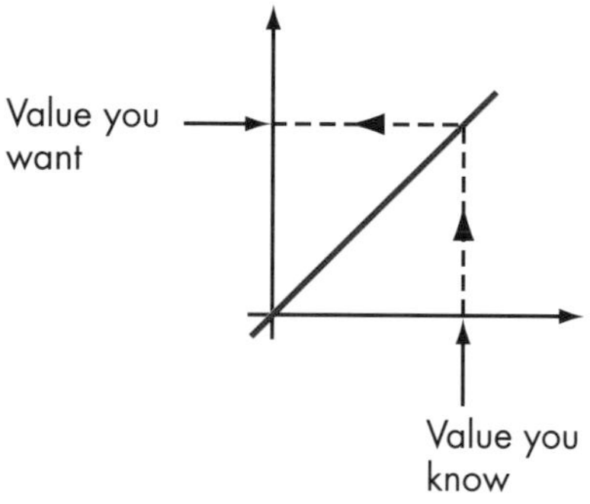

Value you want

Value you know

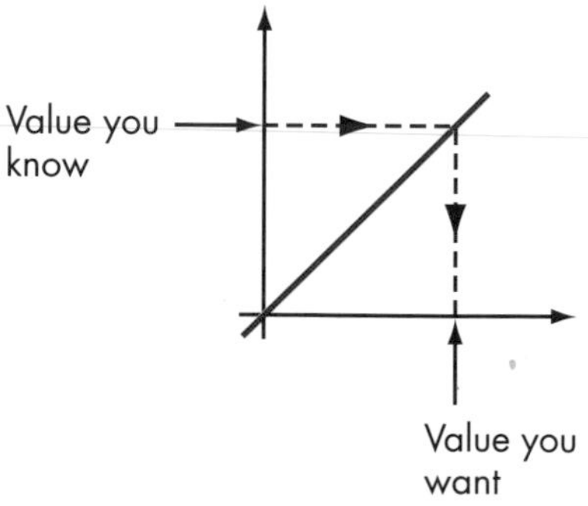

Value you know

Value you want

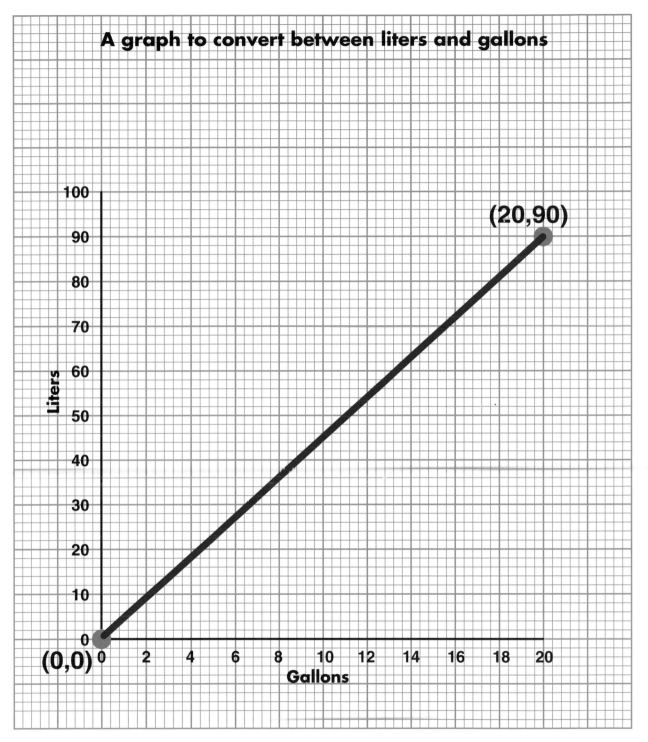

**A graph to convert between liters and gallons**

(20,90)

Liters

100
90
80
70
60
50
40
30
20
10
0

(0,0)

0  2  4  6  8  10  12  14  16  18  20

**Gallons**

**Remember...** You only need two points to draw a straight line. Find the easiest point you can by putting 0 on one side of the equation.

**Word check**

**Convert:** To change one measurement system into another.

**Note...** This graph has been constructed accurately so that you can use it for converting between gallons and liters even if you do not want to make a graph for yourself.

# Kilometers and miles

Here is a graph that allows you to convert between kilometers and miles.

## Setting up the graph

The equation you need to know for this conversion is:

## 1 mile = 1.6 kilometers

We know that 0 miles must also be 0 kilometers, so the line must go through the origin point (0,0).

If 1 mile = 1.6 kilometers, then 10 miles is 16 kilometers, and this gives us the point (10,16).

All you need to draw the graph are these two points.

## Using the graph

To convert from kilometers, start on the kilometer axis. Suppose we want to convert 8 kilometers to miles. Start at 8 and go horizontally until you reach the conversion line. Then go down to the miles line. Read the answer off the miles scale as 5 miles.

To convert from miles to kilometers, do the reverse. To convert 8 miles to kilometers, start on the miles scale. Go up from 8 miles to the conversion line, then across to the kilometer scale. Read the answer as 13 kilometers.

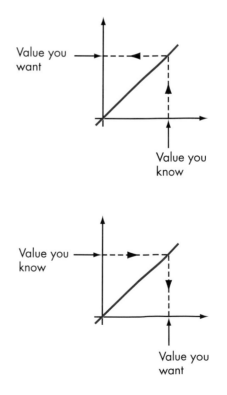

Value you want
Value you know

Value you know
Value you want

# A graph to convert between kilometers and miles

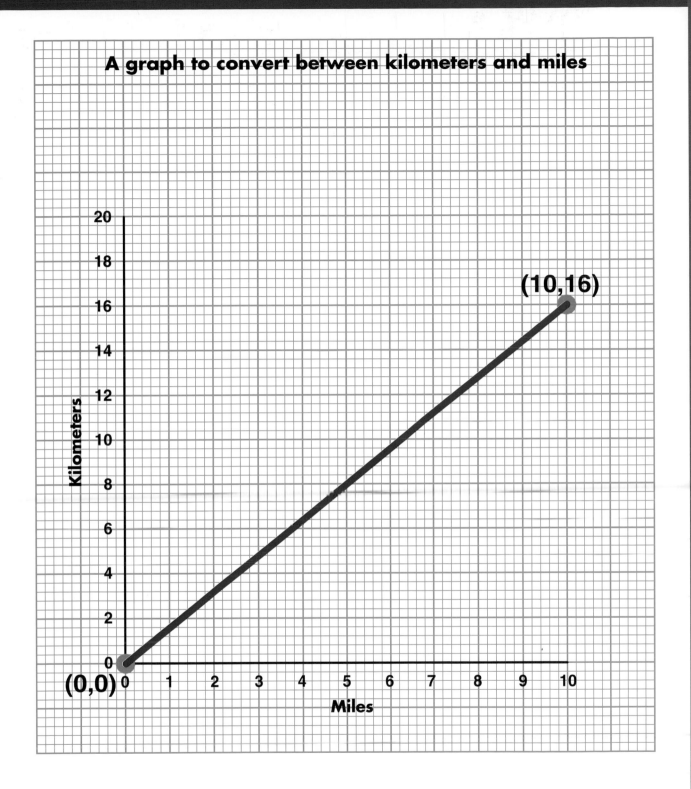

(10,16)

Kilometers

20
18
16
14
12
10
8
6
4
2
0

(0,0) 0    1    2    3    4    5    6    7    8    9    10

Miles

# Centimeters and inches

Here is a graph that allows you to convert between centimeters and inches. It is different from the one on the previous page because, in general, we need to convert between parts of an inch and parts of a centimeter. So, in this case, we have to learn how to read decimal numbers from a chart.

## Setting up the graph

The equation you need to know for this conversion is:

$$\textbf{1 inch = 2.54 cm}$$

Because **0** inches is also **0** centimeters, the line goes through the origin at point (0,0).

1 inch is **2.54** cm, point (**1**, **2.54**) (notice that this is a decimal number).

10 inches is (**10** × **2.54** =) **25.4** cm, point (**10**, **25.4**).

We can now use these two points to produce a graph that converts between **0** and about **12** inches (**1** foot), the sort of range you would want when converting, say, between the sizes of things you might buy in a shop.

## Using the graph

To convert from centimeters, start on the centimeter axis. Suppose we want to convert **4.0** centimeters to inches. Start at **4.0**, and go horizontally until you reach the conversion line. Then, go down to the inches line. Read the answer off the inches axis as **1.6** inches.

To convert from inches to centimeters, do the reverse. To convert **7** inches, start on the inches scale, and go up to the conversion line, then across to the centimeters scale. Read the answer as **17.8** centimeters.

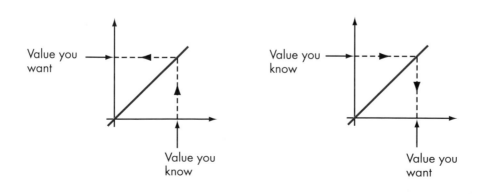

Value you want

Value you know

Value you know

Value you want

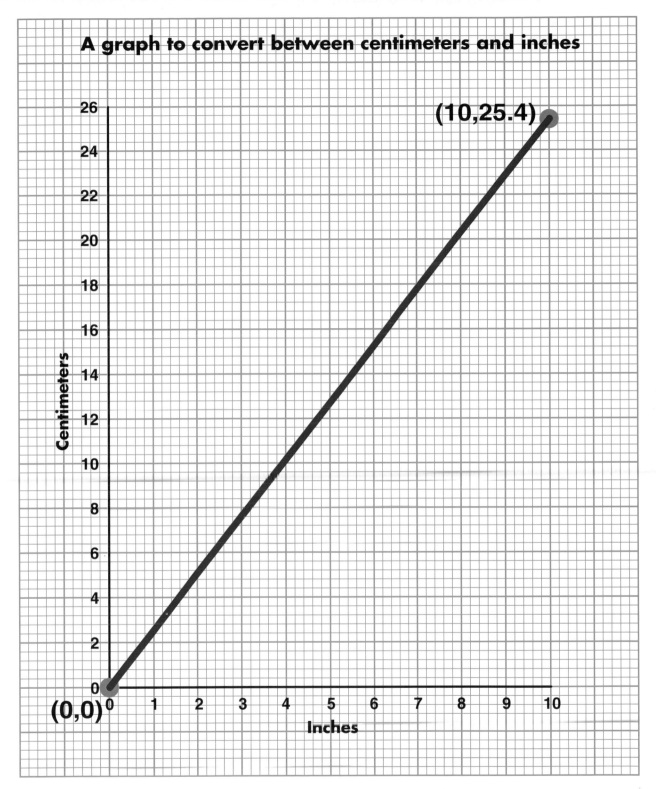

# A graph to convert between centimeters and inches

(10,25.4)

Centimeters

(0,0)

Inches

Word check

**Decimal number:** A number that contains parts of units as well as whole units. The decimal point is used to separate the units from the parts of a unit.

# Kilograms and pounds

This is a graph that converts between kilograms and pounds in weight. It also uses decimal numbers

## Setting up the graph

The equation you need to know for this conversion is:

## 1 kilogram = 2.2 pounds

Clearly 0 kilograms is also 0 pounds, so the line goes through the origin, point (0,0).

5 kilograms is (5 × 2.2 =) 11 pounds; plot this as the second point (11,5).

We can now use these two points to produce a graph that converts between 0 and about 6 kilograms, the sort of range you would need when converting, say, food weights in a recipe book.

## Using the graph

To convert from kilograms, start with the value you want to convert on the kilograms scale. For example, if we want to convert 2.8 kilograms, start at 2.8 and go horizontally until you reach the conversion line. Then go down to the pounds line. Read the answer off the pounds axis as 6.2 pounds.

To convert from pounds to kilos, do the reverse. If we want to convert 10 pounds to kilograms, then we start on the pounds line and move up to the conversion line, then cross to the kilograms line. Read off the answer as 4.55 kilograms.

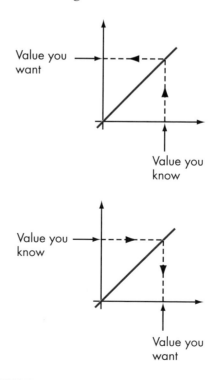

Value you want

Value you know

Value you know

Value you want

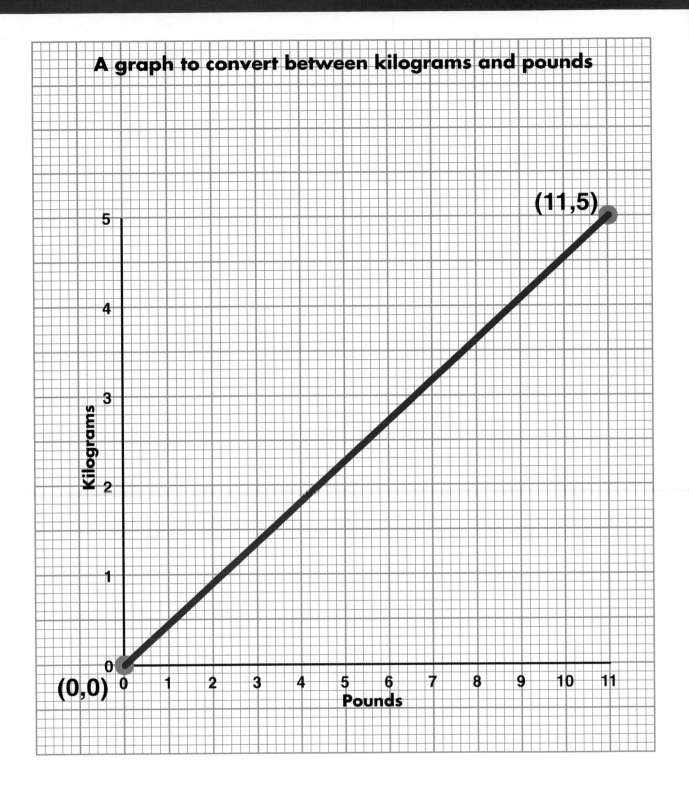

## A graph to convert between kilograms and pounds

(11,5)

Kilograms

5

4

3

2

1

0

(0,0)  0    1    2    3    4    5    6    7    8    9    10   11

**Pounds**

**Book link...** To find out more about decimals, see the book *Decimals* in the *Math Matters!* Set.

**Scales...** Note that in this example we are not using whole numbers. This is because the scale only runs over a small range of weights. So the answers we get are often decimals.

# Celsius and Fahrenheit

There are two main scales for measuring temperature (**T**). Here is a conversion graph that can be used below freezing too. In Celsius these are all minus temperatures. But in Fahrenheit they are not always so.

The conversion formula is: $$T°F = \frac{9 \times T°C}{5} + 32$$

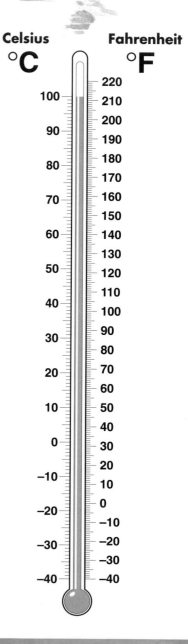

## How hot is it there?

Shane and Joe were e-mail buddies. Shane lived in Brisbane, Australia, Joe lived in Chicago. They often used to tell each other about the weather, but while Shane used Celsius, Joe used Fahrenheit. The only solution was to have some kind of conversion that they could both use.

The first type of conversion they tried was a conversion diagram, like the one on the right.

But there was another way. They could make a conversion graph. Shane drew two thermometers at right angles that crossed each other at their zero marks, Celsius across the page, and Fahrenheit up. Both were marked out from −40° to boiling point.

Now using the formula when T°C is 0, T°F is 32, he could plot the point (0,32).

And when T°C = −40, T°F is also −40, so he could plot the point (−40,−40) (although any other point calculated from the formula would have done just as well).

Finally, he took a ruler and joined the two dots together.

Looking carefully at this graph, Shane could see that the line allowed him to convert between the Celsius temperatures and the Fahrenheit temperatures in the same way as reading from one scale to another on the thermometer.

# A graph to convert between Fahrenheit and Celsius

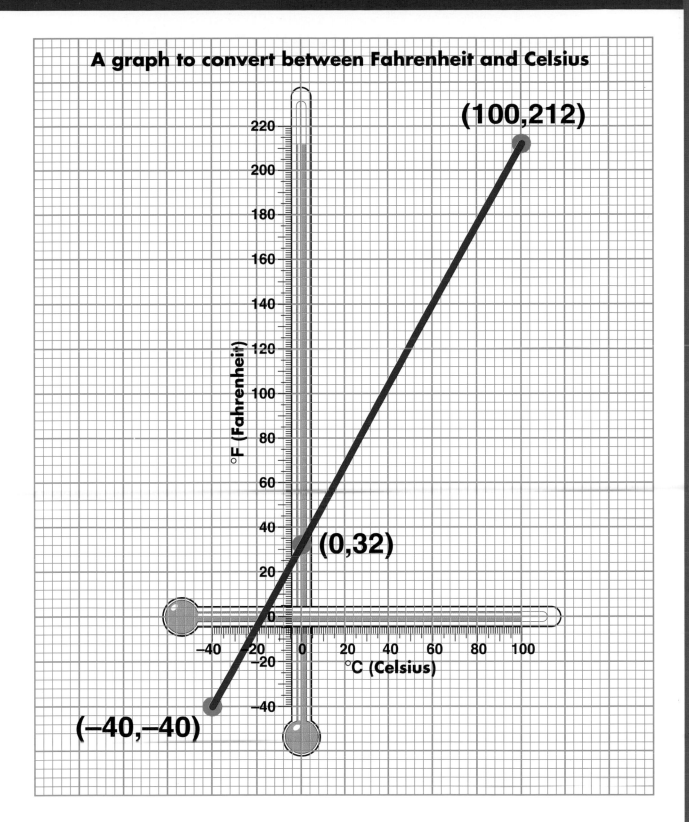

(100,212)

(0,32)

(−40,−40)

°F (Fahrenheit)

°C (Celsius)

**Remember...** The temperature scales are related, but they are not proportional because the line does not pass through the origin.

**Book link...** Find out more about how graphs work in the book *Tables and Charts*, and find out more about proportion in the book *Fractions* in the *Math Matters!* set.

# Lines that connect different things

A straight-line graph can be used to connect two different kinds of measurement – distance and time.

The story below can easily be shown on a graph, as you will see.

## Slow and steady wins the race

Ferdy challenged Juan to a race. Ferdy was fast and a bit conceited too. Juan was not a fast runner, but he was steady and reliable. He agreed to try.

They both set off as fast as they could, and Ferdy was soon out of sight. Glancing around, he could not see Juan, but he did see a friend, so he stopped for a chat.

Ferdy was so interested in what his friend was saying that he did not notice Juan go jogging past. Eventually Ferdy remembered the time and started running again, but he had left it too late.

## Graphing the race

Let's look at how the race can be shown on a graph. The graph opposite shows time on the bottom axis and distance on the upright axis. When each runner is running, the distance he covers is proportional to how much time he has been running. This can be shown as a straight sloping line on a graph. The steeper the slope of the line, the more distance is covered per minute, so the faster the runner is going.

At the beginning of the race the runners have traveled no distance, so the line goes through the origin (0,0).

**Step 1:** Ferdy runs faster, so he is shown as a steeper line than Juan.

**Step 2:** When Ferdy stops for a chat, the time continues, but he doesn't cover any distance. Notice that this is shown by a level piece of the line.

This is the stage when Juan overtakes Ferdy.

**Step 3:** Ferdy starts to run again, so his line has the same slope as in step 1. But he has left it too late, and Juan reaches the finish line first.

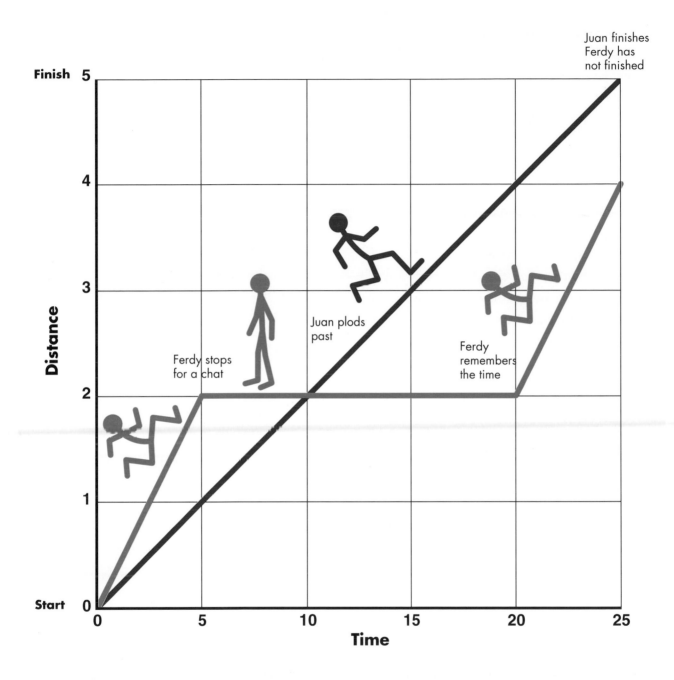

Juan finishes
Ferdy has
not finished

**Finish** 5

4

**Distance**

3

Ferdy stops
for a chat

Juan plods
past

Ferdy
remembers
the time

2

1

**Start** 0

0    5    10    15    20    25

**Time**

**Remember...** You can use a graph to show relationships between things far more clearly than in a description.

**Book link...** To find out more about proportion, see the book *Fractions* in the *Math Matters!* set.

# Using a line graph to solve problems

Line graphs are an excellent way of solving problems. This example will show you how to do it.

## The dripping pipe

Just two days before Fred and Mavis went on vacation, Mavis noticed a damp patch on the bathroom carpet. She called Fred to look at it. Oh no! one of their water pipes was leaking.

Fred put a large coffee can underneath to catch the drips and to work out how bad the leak was. **6** hours later there was ¼ inch of water in the can. **12** hours from the start there was ½ inch. **18** hours later Fred was asleep, but **24** hours (**1** day) from the start there was **1** inch of water in the can.

They were going away for a week, and since it was now Sunday, it would be difficult and expensive to get a plumber to call to fix the leak. The can was 7½ inches deep.

Fred figured that the leak appeared to be dripping regularly at **1** inch per day. So, if he emptied the can just before they left, then in **7** days it would fill up **7 × 1 = 7** inches, and they would be able to call a plumber when they returned home.

## The line graph

You can use a line graph to solve this problem easily. Just plot the points and join them up, as has been done in the graph on page 41. It is fair to join up the plotted points and extend the line to show what will happen in **7** days.

As you can see, the can will fill to **7** inches over **7** days, so Fred will just get back in time before the can spills over.

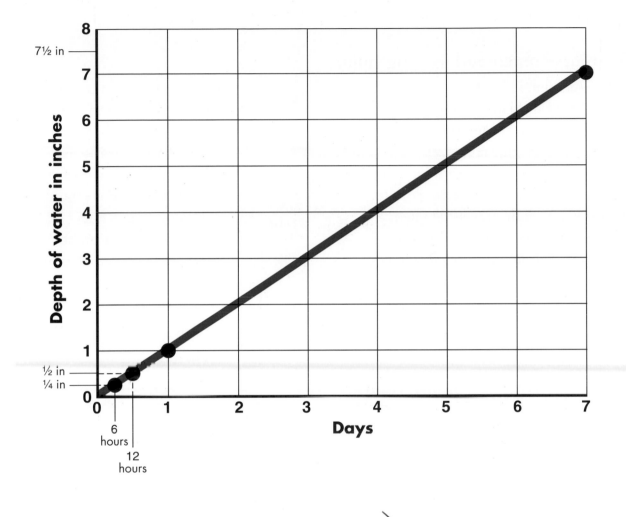

Remember... Graphs are often useful
for explaining your answer, even when
you can solve a problem without them.

# Solving problems with two lines

Line graphs can solve some problems
very easily, as this example shows.

## Climbing Romeo and jogging Juliet

Romeo sets out at 9 a.m. to
climb 5 miles up a mountain to
Juliet's house. He climbs at 1
mile per hour (mph). He never
arrives, because at 10 a.m. Juliet
acts on her own idea of jogging
down the mountain to visit Romeo.
She jogs down at 4 mph. When do
they meet? And how far has Romeo
climbed by then?

## How to draw the lines

In this case we need to draw two
lines, one for Romeo and one for
Juliet. Notice that in this case
we wouldn't want to start
the graphs at 0 (midnight)
because we would have a
lot of wasted paper. So
the graphs start at 9 a.m.

We can plot two
points to draw a line
for Romeo: his starting
point (9,0) and (10,1)
because he climbs
one mile in 1 hour.
Then we join up the
points and extend the
line to the right.

Our starting point for Juliet
is (10,5) (10 a.m. and 5 miles
from Romeo). She jogs 4
miles in an hour toward
Romeo (i.e., downward),
so another point would be
11 a.m. and 1 mile (11,1).
Join these two points.
As you will see, the lines
cross, and this is the
answer, where they meet.

## What the graph shows

The graph uses 5 large
squares for each hour on
the bottom line, so Romeo
and Juliet meet at exactly 9
squares across. That is, 1 hour
and $\frac{4}{5}$ th of another hour after 9 a.m.
One fifth of an hour is $\frac{60}{5} = 12$
minutes, so they meet at 12 minutes
to 11 o'clock, or 10:48 a.m.

Since Romeo has been climbing at
1 mile every hour, by the time they
meet he will have climbed 1.8 of the
5 miles to Juliet's house. Because we
use 10 small squares to every mile on
the upright scale, you can find this
from the graph too.

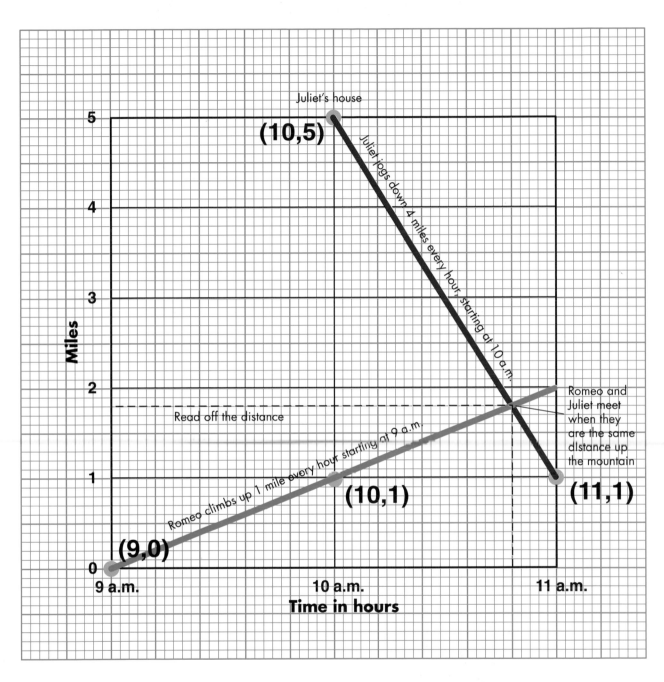

Juliet's house

**(10,5)**

Juliet jogs down 4 miles every hour, starting at 10 a.m.

5

4

3

**Miles**

2

Read off the distance

Romeo and Juliet meet when they are the same distance up the mountain

Romeo climbs up 1 mile every hour starting at 9 a.m.

1

**(10,1)**

**(11,1)**

**(9,0)**

0

9 a.m.

10 a.m.

11 a.m.

**Time in hours**

**Remember…** You can use two lines to solve some tricky problems.

# What symbols mean

Here is a list of the common math symbols together with an example of how they are used. You will find this list in each of the *Math Matters!* books, so that you can turn to any book if you want to look up the meaning of a symbol.

**—** Between two numbers this symbol means "subtract" or "minus." In front of one number it means the number is negative. In Latin *minus* means "less."

**+** The symbol for adding. We say it "plus." In Latin *plus* means "more."

**✕** The symbol for multiplying. We say it "multiplied by" or "times."

**=** The symbol fo r equals. We say it "equals" or "makes." It comes from a Latin word meaning "level" because weighing scales are level when the amounts on each side are equal.

$$(8 + 9 - 3) \times \frac{2}{5} = 5.6$$

**( )** Parentheses. You do everything inside the parentheses first. Parentheses always occur in pairs.

**—, /,** and **÷** Three symbols for dividing. We say it "divided by." A pair of numbers above and below a / or — make a fraction, so ⅖ or $\frac{2}{5}$ is the fraction two-fifths.

**■** This is a decimal point. It is a dot written after the units when a number contains parts of a unit as well as whole numbers. This is the decimal number five point six or five and six-tenths.

# Glossary

*Terms commonly used in this book.*

**Axes:** The zero lines on a grid. The x-axis is across. The y-axis is up.

**Continuous:** A number scale that increases smoothly, without jumps or steps.

**Convert:** To change one measurement system into another.

**Coordinates:** The pair of numbers that tells you the position of a point on a graph. They are usually enclosed by parentheses.

**Decimal number:** A number that contains parts of units as well as whole units. The decimal point is used to separate the units from the parts of a unit.

**Degree:** A small part of a complete turn. There are 360 degrees in a complete turn.

**Equation:** A number sentence using the = symbol, telling us that two different ways of writing a number are the same. For example, $2 + 2 = 4$ and $9 - 5 = 4$.

**Grid:** A pattern of lines that cross at right angles and are used to make it easier to write down your work.

**Horizontal:** Level and flat, like the surface of still water.

**Intercept:** The point where a line graph crosses the y-axis. It is the amount the line is lifted above a parallel line through the origin.

**Latitude:** Lines drawn on a map or globe parallel to the equator. They are measured in angles north or south, for example, 52°N.

**Longitude:** Angles that mark the distance of places east or west of Greenwich.

**Map:** A scale drawing of a place.

**Mental map:** A map of a place that you know well and that you keep in your head.

**Minus numbers:** The numbers that fall below zero on a number line (scale). Minus numbers or zero cannot be used for counting, only for measuring things like temperature. Minus numbers are also called negative numbers.

**Ordered pair:** Any pair of things (such as coordinates, for example) in which the order matters.

**Origin:** The point where the axes of a graph cross.

**Pair:** Two things that match up in some way.

**Parallel:** Parallel lines are lines that remain the same distance apart forever.

**Proportion:** A comparative share in something.

**Right angle:** An angle that is exactly a quarter of a complete turn.

**Sector:** A piece of a circle, like a piece of a pie.

**Single-digit number:** A number between 0 and 9.

**Slope:** A surface or line that is not level. How much (or steeply) it goes up is measured by the ratio UP:ACROSS.

**Vertical:** Upright, perpendicular to the horizontal.

# Set index